Designing your
TAX-SMART RETIREMENT INCOME PLAN

DAN MORRIS

MCMF Publishing

COPYRIGHT © 2024 by Dan Morris

All rights reserved. No part of this book may be used or reproduced in any manner whatsoever without prior written consent of the author, except as provided by the United States of America copyright law.

Published by MCMF Publishing

Disclaimer

This publication is designed to provide accurate and authoritative information in regard to the subject matter covered. It is sold with the understanding that neither the author nor the publisher is engaged in rendering legal, investment, accounting, or other professional services. While the publisher and author have used their best efforts in preparing this book, they make no representations or warranties with respect to the accuracy or completeness of the contents of this book and specifically disclaim any implied warranties of merchantability or fitness for a particular purpose. No warranty may be created or extended by sales representatives or written sales materials. The advice and strategies contained herein may not be suitable for your situation. You should consult with a professional when appropriate. Neither the publisher nor the author shall be liable for any loss of profit or any other commercial damages, including but not limited to special, incidental, consequential, personal, or other damages.

Contents

Dedication	1
Foreword by Barry Brooksby	3
Foreword by Craig R. Cheney	5
Part 1 - Welcome	7
Who This Book Is For	9
My Promise to You	13
Introduction	17
Part 2 - Designing a Tax-Smart Retirement Income Plan	21
1. The Foundation: Why Creating a Written Retirement Income Plan Matters	23
2. Bridging the Gap Part 1: Accumulation vs. Distribution Planning	35

3. Bridging the Gap Part 2: Strategies to Maintain and Increase Retirement Income	43
4. Smart Planning for a Prosperous Retirement	53
5. Protecting Retirement Income from Taxes	65
6. Medicare and IRMAA: Navigating Healthcare Traps in Retirement	73
7. Supercharging Income: Maximizing Social Security Benefits	81
Conclusion:	89
Part 3 - The Next Step	91
8. The Next Steps	93
Resources & Social Media	97
About The Author	99
Fullpage image	102

Dedication

I want to express my heartfelt gratitude to my Dad, Russell J. Morris, for his unwavering belief in me and his encouragement to assist others with their retirement income plans. Though our time together on his retirement income plan was brief, I truly valued the experience. My Dad discovered the significance of managing his diabetes later in life, a lesson I carry with me. If he were here today, he would emphasize, "Your health is vital for a fulfilling life and retirement." So, I urge everyone to prioritize and maintain a healthy lifestyle, as true wealth lies in good health.

Thank You

In the past few years, I have collaborated with numerous individuals to refine and enrich this book with valuable insights. I aimed to share the real-life stories of those I've had the privilege to work with. Thank you to each of you—you know who you are. I honestly couldn't have accomplished this without your support. Additionally, I included members of my dad's family, who are now in their 70s and 80s.

From the outset, I sought feedback from senior citizens in my family, as they inspired me to write this book. Their dedication to providing for their families and saving for retirement is remarkable. It takes a lifetime to accomplish these two significant tasks, raising a family and planning for retirement. Therefore, I extend special thanks to my uncle Gordon and his wife Leslie, my aunts Marilyn and Roberta, and Uncle Lon, Roberta's husband. Your feedback and encouragement have meant the world to me, and I cherish all of you.

Foreword by Barry Brooksby

"Dan Morris is *the* IRMAA Expert, with knowledge and experience. His years of experience have allowed him to work with people throughout the country on keeping more of their money. As Robert Kiyoski said in his book Rich Dad Poor Dad, it's not just about the money you make, it's about the money you keep.

Dan does a remarkable job of helping people fix the money leaks in their financial lives and hold onto more money. If you don't plan for your retirement future, chances are you'll be left with less money than you could have had. One of the ways Dan teaches people to plan is with the foundational asset of High Cash Value Whole Life Insurance. The reason Dan recommends high cash value whole life insurance is because of the many benefits a whole life policy provides to pre-retirees and retirees alike. Not only do these high cash value whole life policies provide guaranteed growth of a person's money and access to liquid cash prior to age 59 ½ without a penalty, but they also provide people with tax-free retirement income. Tax-free income in retirement can be a game changer because no one, not even the best financial adviser out there, knows what future tax rates will be. The more tax-free income you have in retirement, the better.

Dan will teach you about this foundational asset of High Cash Value Whole Life Insurance and show you the tax-free retirement income that you can have in your retirement years. High Cash Value Whole Life Insurance is an asset that will enhance your overall portfolio, financial life and retirement."

Barry Brooksby- Founder/CEO of Focus Wealth Group
https://FocusWealthGroup.com

Foreword by Craig R. Cheney

Most Financial and Retirement Income Advisors like to say IRMAA is a "pesky little charge". Let's look... let's say one has a $300k in a 401k account and $300k in stock market brokerage account for a married couple. Let's assume a whopping 9% return every year ($45k) which will put them into Medicare and IRMAA (4th bracket) and reduce that return by 28%. This will also reduce the overall net return to only 6.42% and that is before further erosion by capital gains taxes or RMDs or higher Social Security Income taxes.

Dan will assist you mitigate your retirement income plan from future income taxes and any possible IRMAA surcharges.

Craig R. Cheney – President/Cee Way Solutions
www.ceewaysolutions.com

*"Age is an issue of mind over matter.
If you don't mind, it doesn't matter."*

Mark Twain

Part 1
WELCOME

"The biggest adventure you can take is to live the life of your dreams."

Oprah Winfrey

Who This Book Is For

If you're flipping through these pages, you're likely standing at the beginning of a new chapter in your life—retirement. Perhaps you've spent decades building a successful career, diligently saving for this moment, but now find yourself wondering if you're truly prepared for what lies ahead. You're eager to embrace the freedom and relaxation that retirement promises, yet a nagging worry persists: will your hard-earned savings last as long as you do?

This book is tailored for individuals between 55 and 70 who have accumulated a fair amount of savings and are either on the cusp of retirement or have recently stepped into this new phase of life. This guide is designed to help you navigate the transition from accumulating wealth to effectively distributing it in retirement.

You might have a good grasp of basic financial concepts but find yourself overwhelmed by the intricacies of retirement planning. The landscape has changed dramatically in recent years, with new regulations and laws reshaping the retirement planning landscape. Many haven't kept pace with these changes, leaving their retirement strategies outdated and potentially inadequate.

Throughout these pages, we'll tackle the challenges that keep you up at night:

1. Making your savings last a lifetime

2. Managing and minimizing healthcare costs

3. Optimizing your Social Security benefits

4. Navigating the tax implications of retirement income

5. Balancing the need for growth with your desire for financial security

You'll find this book packed with practical advice and actionable strategies. We'll demystify complex topics like Medicare, Individual Retirement Accounts (IRAs) and IRMAA (Income-Related Monthly Adjustment Amount), explaining them in clear, understandable terms. You'll learn about innovative approaches like "Inflation

Kicker Accounts" and smart tax strategies that can help you keep more of your hard-earned money.

For those of you who are married, we'll explore strategies that benefit both spouses. And if leaving a legacy for your children or grandchildren is important to you, we'll cover that too.

This isn't just about crunching numbers—it's about helping you envision and achieve a retirement where you're free to enjoy life without constant financial worry. We'll look at how to maintain your quality of life, maximize your income and even explore fulfilling ways to stay engaged and potentially earn during retirement.

Remember, you're not alone in this journey. Just as you consult a doctor about your health, this book encourages you to seek expert guidance in optimizing your retirement strategy. We'll show you how to leverage technology and professional expertise to create a retirement plan that's as unique as you are.

"Happiness is not a station you arrive at, but a manner of traveling."

Margaret Lee Runbeck

My Promise to You

Imagine you're sitting on your porch, sipping your morning coffee, watching the sunrise. There's no rush to get to work, no stress about deadlines. This is retirement - the golden years you've worked so hard to reach. But here's the million-dollar question: Are you confident that this peaceful scene can last for 20, 30, or even 40 years?

That's where I come in. I'm not just another financial advisor spouting textbook theories. I've been in the trenches for over two decades, building businesses, navigating market ups and downs and helping countless individuals turn their retirement dreams into reality. My journey has taught me that retirement planning isn't just about saving money - it's about making that money work tirelessly for you when you're ready to relax.

Here's what I bring to the table:

1. **Battle-Tested Strategies**: My advice isn't just

theory - it's backed by years of real-world experience. I've seen what works and what doesn't in the ever-changing landscape of retirement planning.

2. **Tax-Savvy Approaches**: I'll show you how to keep more of your hard-earned money in your pocket and out of Uncle Sam's. We'll explore tax-free wealth-building strategies that can make a significant difference in your retirement income.

3. **Healthcare Cost Navigation**: Let's face it - healthcare can be a major expense in retirement. I'll guide you through the maze of Medicare, help you understand those tricky IRMAA surcharges and show you how to plan for potential long-term care needs.

4. **Social Security Optimization**: We'll time your benefits just right to maximize this crucial piece of your retirement puzzle.

5. **Inflation-Beating Techniques**: Ever heard of Inflation Kicker Accounts? You will. I'll show you how to ensure your purchasing power stays strong, even as the years go by.

6. **Legacy Planning**: If leaving something for the next generation is important to you, we've got that covered, too.

I promise to explain all of this in plain English. No financial jargon, no complex formulas - just straightforward, actionable advice that you can understand and implement.

This book isn't just a one-time read. Consider it your retirement planning companion - a resource you'll return to again and again as you navigate this new chapter of your life.

Remember, you wouldn't embark on a cross-country road trip without a map. Think of this book as your GPS for the retirement journey. I'll help you avoid the potholes, navigate the detours and find the scenic routes to your ideal retirement.

So, are you ready to turn that peaceful porch scene from a fleeting moment into a lasting reality? Let's roll up our sleeves and craft a retirement plan that's as unique as you are. Together, we'll transform your hard-earned savings into a stream of retirement income that can weather any storm.

Introduction

Imagine sitting across from your father, his eyes filled with trust and uncertainty, as he asks for your help with a decision that could impact the rest of his life. That was me in 2003, when my dad, at 61, turned to me for advice on when to start his Social Security benefits. Little did I know that this conversation would not only change his life but set me on a path that would define my career and purpose.

My father had been battling diabetes since he was 42, a fact that loomed large in our discussion. This health challenge added a layer of complexity to our decision. As I dove into research, consulting retirement experts and poring over Social Security guidelines, I realized this wasn't just about numbers on a page. It was about ensuring my dad could enjoy his golden years with financial peace of mind despite his health challenges.

After careful consideration, I advised him to start his benefits at 62. It wasn't conventional wisdom, but it was right for him. The relief in his eyes when I explained my reasoning is something I'll never forget. It was a moment that underscored the power of personalized, thoughtful financial advice.

Tragically, my father passed away in 2011 at the age of 68; his life was cut short by complications from diabetes. In our final conversations, he expressed gratitude for the advice I'd given him years earlier. His words of encouragement, urging me to pursue retirement planning, became a guiding light in my career.

Losing him was devastating, but it ignited a fire within me. I realized that my dad's story wasn't unique. Countless others were facing similar challenges, navigating the complex waters of retirement planning with health concerns and financial uncertainties. I couldn't change the past for my dad, but I could honor his memory by helping others secure their financial futures.

As I dedicated myself to this mission, I uncovered a critical gap in the industry. Many were focused solely on accumulating wealth, overlooking the crucial phase of distributing those savings effectively in retirement. For instance, taxes in retirement were often underestimated. And there was another surprise lurking: many retirees were shocked to discover that their Medicare premiums could suddenly increase based on their income. This is due to something called IRMAA - a government policy that can significantly raise healthcare costs for higher-income retirees. These factors, if not properly planned for, could seriously impact on the comfort and security people had worked so hard to achieve in retirement.

My commitment to helping others with their retirement income planning was put to the test during the 2008 financial crisis. This event further cemented my understanding of financial resilience. As I guided clients through those turbulent times, I gained invaluable insights into creating robust retirement strategies that could weather economic storms.

Now, I'm here to share these insights with you. Just as I did for my father, I'll guide you through innovative approaches to generating retirement income. We'll tackle how to adapt your plan when life throws curveballs - because, believe me, it will. And just as importantly, we'll delve into ways to find purpose and fulfillment in your retirement years because retirement is about more than just money.

It's time to take proactive steps toward securing your future. Your golden years should be just that—golden. Let's work together to make that a reality.

*"Happiness is not something ready made.
It comes from your own actions."*

Dalai Lama

Part 2
DESIGNING A TAX-SMART RETIREMENT INCOME PLAN

"In the end, it's not the years in your life that count. It's the life in your years."

Abraham Lincoln

Chapter One

The Foundation: Why Creating a Written Retirement Income Plan Matters

In life, we often take the time to plan out the big events—our education, buying our dream house, those once-in-a-lifetime vacations and even our wedding days. However, when we get to retirement, a stage that could easily span a third of our lives, many of us don't put the same effort or detail into planning. As someone approaching or in your early retirement years, you may find yourself in this position. I've seen this time and time again as an advisor, and it's become a significant part of my mission to raise awareness of the importance of a written Retirement Income Plan.

Think about what it would be like trying to build a house without detailed building plans. The confusion, the financial setbacks, no research on the related rules, the unstable foundation—these issues are not something you'd want to encounter in retirement. And that's precisely the kind of situation people find themselves in when they step into retirement without a clear, written plan. The key to making retirement planning work is focusing on something simple that gets overlooked too often—INCOME, INCOME & MORE INCOME!

Having a successful retirement can no longer just be focused on accumulating assets. It has to ensure the money that hits your bank account every month is enough and keeps coming, alongside being managed with the right laws in mind that can affect the final total. For example, I've met plenty of people just like you who only look at their gross income and fail to plan for income tax and IRMAA surcharges or how to keep their wealth growing tax-free. This kind of oversight can really impact the retirement life you're working toward and result in fewer funds to live on and a different future for your retirement than what you may have imagined.

A pertinent example - IRMAA, or the Income-Related Monthly Adjustment Amount can be a significant curveball for many entering retirement. It affects how much you'll pay for Medicare Part B and Part D[1], Insurance and how your retirement income can unexpectedly increase your healthcare costs. Many people aren't aware of this and it can significantly reduce the retirement comfort they were counting on. If you're between 55-70 years old, this is something you need to understand now, before it impacts your retirement plans. However, once you understand the circumstances surrounding it and with that knowledge, it is crucial to manage your wealth strategically by exploring tax-free options. This example is one of the many that can affect your plans for when the days of working are behind you. We'll get into more details on IRMAA in Chapter 6, but for now, I've got a story that perfectly illustrates why writing down your retirement plan can be the best way to avoid financial challenges during retirement.

---

1. There are four parts of Medicare: Part A, Part B, Part C, and Part D. Part A provides inpatient/hospital coverage. Part B provides outpatient/medical coverage. Part C offers an alternate way to receive your Medicare benefits (see below for more information). Part D provides prescription drug coverage.

An Unpleasant Surprise

A while back, I met a couple, James and Clara[2], who were doing quite well financially for themselves with a portfolio of rental properties in their possession. Financially savvy and with a CPA at their disposal, they thought they had their finances figured out. But there was a complication they hadn't caught – the impact of IRMAA surcharges on their income. Despite having professional help, the world of IRMAA and its effect on Medicare deductions from Social Security income was off their radar. And it was no small oversight; with their income placing them in a high IRMAA bracket, they were facing about $3.5 million in projected Medicare surcharges over a 30-year retirement. This was a significant financial burden. That was when they reached out to me.

Taking a comprehensive approach, we began reshaping their retirement income plan. It wasn't an immediate solution; placing them in a different and more manageable IRMAA bracket took a few years. The key component of our strategy was an IRMAA income test – something we run for all our clients. This forecasts future IRMAA

---

2. Their names and all others mentioned, and specific details of their story, were changed to keep their identities private.

surcharges and uses this insight to guide clients like James and Clara towards more efficient, tax-efficient moves, like shifting funds to Tax-Free or Tax-Advantage accounts.

The payoff was a significant amount of dollars saved, resulting in improved financial security. Thanks to them reaching out for help, they now have a retirement plan that truly matches their needs. And the word spread. Before long, referrals from their circle began coming my way, each looking to secure their retirement income against unforeseen IRMAA Medicare surcharges and high-income tax brackets.

I wanted to share their story because it's a valuable reminder of the unpredictable situations that can impact even the most knowledgeable investor's retirement plans and the importance of expert guidance to navigate them. I keep returning to their path from feeling uncertain to fully in charge. Retirement planning can get complex with all its intricacies, but if you've got a solid plan you can actually read and understand, navigating becomes much easier.

In more practical terms, your plan can be extensive, but it doesn't have to be complicated. It should cover everything – how taxes are going to affect your income, sorting out healthcare, getting the most out of Social Security and dealing with life's unexpected events. It's like putting together a comprehensive strategy of retirement, making sure you're looking at the whole picture, ready for the challenges and identifying opportunities.

So, what's the key to a retirement plan that covers all the bases? Let me give you an overview into my Pyramid Retirement Planning Steps. This is the result of years spent guiding people through the retirement planning landscape, reducing the confusion and crafting a path that's clear and easy to follow:

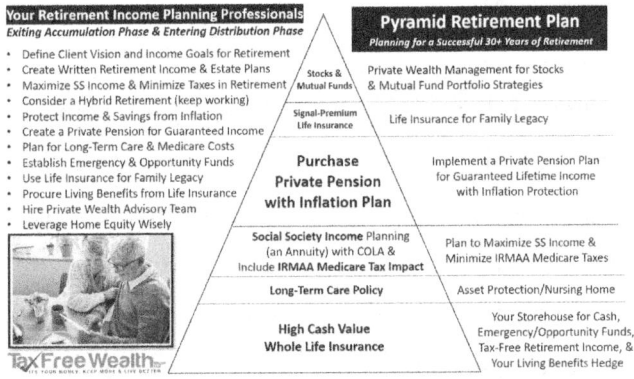

Steps to the best plan possible:

1. **What's Your Dream Retirement Look Like?**
   First up, envision your ideal retirement. What are you doing? Where are you living? And, importantly, how much income will you need to make

this happen?

2. **Get It Down on Paper:** We're talking about a detailed strategy that covers the cash flow you'll need and how you plan to pass on what's left to the people you care about.

3. **Boosting Social Security and Tackling Taxes:** We'll figure out how to maximize those Social Security checks and keep the tax burden at bay so you can keep more of your hard-earned money.

4. **Mixing Work and Play:** Have you ever considered a semi-retirement? For those of you who aren't quite ready to fully retire, it keeps some money coming in and provides structure while still giving you plenty of free time.

5. **Inflation-Proofing Your Wallet:** Let's make sure your money keeps up with the cost of living so you can still afford a comfortable life ten, twenty or thirty years down the line.

6. **Creating Your Own Pension:** We'll explore how annuities or other strategies can give you a paycheck every month, consistently.

7. **Healthcare Without the Headaches:** Let's plan now for those future medical bills to keep them from catching you off guard or depleting your savings. This is especially crucial as healthcare costs tend to rise as we age.

8. **Rainy Day and Dream Fund:** You'll want some funds you can easily access for unexpected expenses or discretionary spending.

9. **Leaving a Legacy with Life Insurance:** The challenging conversation of imagining a world where you are no longer present can be difficult, but life insurance can be a strategic way to leave something behind for your loved ones.

10. **Smart Home Equity Moves:** Your home could be a valuable asset for funding retirement. Let's talk downsizing, reverse mortgages and more.

11. **Team Up with the Pros:** Bringing in a wealth advisory team can take your plan to the next level, with advice tailored just for you.

12. **The Perks of Life Insurance You're Still Around to Enjoy:** Beyond the payout when

you're gone, some policies have benefits you can use now.

13. **Leveraging Technology:** We'll explore how user-friendly software and tools can help you stay on top of your retirement plan and make informed decisions.

A solid plan keeps you in the driver's seat. And that's what I'm here for – to help you turn all this complex information about retirement income planning into a clear, actionable plan. Achievable goals, like any dream, must be in written form.

Conclusion

If you reached the end of this chapter feeling concerned that you haven't considered most of the topics we covered, it is okay. As I said before, I wrote these pages to show you what you might not be aware of just yet and offer professional and reliable help with what you will need. Just like James and Clara reached out for help and I managed to improve the situation for them, your story can have a successful outcome, too.

Now, as we move forward, the next two chapters are about one of the most important and concerning aspects of retiring: the income gap. I separated it into two parts to ensure I covered the stories and expertise I must give you for more insight into this aspect of your retirement planning.

"Retirement means doing whatever I want to do. It means choice."

Dianne Nahirny

Chapter Two

Bridging the Gap Part 1: Accumulation vs. Distribution Planning

All through our working lives, we hear it like a mantra: save for retirement. Whether you're working a traditional job or running your own business, this rings true. Yet, an equally important aspect doesn't get its fair share of the spotlight: transitioning from saving money to using it in retirement. While setting aside a portion of your paycheck is step one, the real challenge happens when you figure out how to make that nest egg last and support the retirement lifestyle you've been working for.

In this chapter, I'll explain the why and how of this important transition. When you're armed with the right knowledge and strategic planning, your retirement can be more than just financially stable—it can be enjoyable. The first phase, accumulation, is focused on growing your savings. But without a strategy for distributing those funds—ensuring they last throughout your retirement—reaching your retirement goals might not be as straightforward as you'd hoped.

Golden Years, Guided Paths

One day, a couple named Alex and Emma came to me with questions about retirement planning. They were at a stage where they knew they needed a retirement income plan but were still unsure about the specifics and what steps to take next. Their story is quite illustrative of the challenges many couples face. Alex had a career in the stock market that allowed him to experience market volatility firsthand and was always seeking high-return opportunities. On the other hand, Emma spent her days in the classroom, shaping young minds with a steady hand and a calm spirit. Their views on retirement were as different as night and day, and as a result, their questions were varied but specific.

They avoided addressing their financial future for years, each step taken in the opposite direction. While Alex always trusted his instincts to take more risks for higher returns, Emma was much more conservative and averse to taking larger risks, even for a chance of higher payoffs. As you can probably guess, they reached an impasse—the kind that makes you seriously consider how you're going to move forward.

As a result of their different views, every discussion about money ended in a disagreement, with Alex trusting that the risk in the market would pay off and Emma wanting to take the least amount of risk possible. Vacations, home upgrades and even the weekly grocery list, from time to time, ended up in disagreement. Their financial friction was causing tension in their marriage.

Then came the tipping point. A risky investment Alex was convinced would pay off big went sour, wiping out a significant portion of their savings. For Emma, it was the nightmare she'd always feared and for Alex, a wake-up call about the cost of his risk-taking.

That's when they reached out to me, each one feeling desperate, realizing they needed professional guidance. As I was sitting down with them, the tension was palpable. But here's the thing about facing financial setbacks—it's a solid foundation to start rebuilding.

We started at square one, discussing what retirement meant to each of them. It wasn't easy. There were more than a few intense moments and some tough, soul-searching conversations. But gradually, we bridged their differences.

I introduced them to the idea of balance—not just in their investments but in their lives. We mapped out a plan that gave Alex enough room to invest in the stock market in a way that wouldn't put their future on the line while ensuring Emma's need for security was front and center. The use of annuities, diversified investments, a clear-cut budget for adventures and the everyday unexpected needs—it all came into play.

More than the numbers, though, we worked on communication, on understanding not just the "what" of their disagreements but also the "why." It wasn't a quick fix—real change rarely is—but as their plan took shape, so did a new way of seeing their shared future.

This balancing act between growth potential and security can feel like a tightrope walk. It's tough, right? When one of you is all about the increased returns that come from riskier investments and the other is seeking a haven of safety that brings a smaller return, it's not just challenging; it can strain the very fabric of your relationship. That's where bringing in a neutral third party—an expert who's seen it all and has your best interests at heart—can make all the difference. Finding that middle ground or making informed decisions that respect your desires for growth and security isn't just practical; it can be a relationship saver.

I want this story to remind us that sometimes, reaching out for help is the wisest thing you can do. And finding that balance can be the key to a future you can both look forward to.

The Seven Saturdays Syndrome: The typical financial shift and why you need it now!

Whether you identified more with Alex's risk-tolerant behavior or Emma's risk-averse approach, there is a common misconception about retirement that can affect every retiree, regardless of their personality. When the time comes for you to retire and step into retirement, you're going to find yourself transitioning from being a saver to a spender. It's a shift many folks I've talked to didn't see coming. They thought their spending would reduce once they left the workforce behind. But here's the surprise—every day starts feeling like a Saturday.

Remember those Saturdays when the weekend vibe meant you could do what you wanted and maybe spend a bit because you'd earned it? That's retirement, except it's not just the weekend; it's every single day. And with all this newfound freedom, spending can easily start to increase.

When entering retirement, we need to adapt to a whole new way of life in which every day has the potential for leisure, adventure and, yes, spending.

To tackle this change, you need to craft a personalized spending plan that's as flexible as it is detailed. It's a living document that evolves with your retirement goals, market shifts and those unexpected expenses, giving you a clear picture of the retirement life you're planning. With my clients, I take a holistic approach, partnering up with estate planners to ensure we've covered every angle. This way, we're talking about how to spend your money sustainably and how to keep it safe from unexpected twists and turns life might have in store. We dive deep into making the most of your retirement funds, exploring all the ways to keep taxes low and your income steady. Whether it's Roth conversions, smart asset placement, or just knowing when to withdraw from which account, we're all about stretching every dollar further.

Also, a life full of "Saturdays" combined with aging has to be ready for rising healthcare costs. Spending more on medicine or doctor appointments is bound to happen. We've got to factor in healthcare, Medicare and maybe even long-term care, ensuring those rising costs don't significantly impact your savings. Plus, we look into setting up your own private pension with annuities to add another layer of financial security. Especially for my clients who are business owners, figuring out the next steps can be tricky. Profits don't always follow you into retirement, making the task even harder.

The Goal: Crafting a Future that Fits

We've reached the end of this chapter and I hope I have shown you the importance of having a clear distribution plan for the retirement phase. Imagine if Alex and Emma had structured their plan for the distribution phase more in advance. Their decisions wouldn't have affected their savings so much. Now, think about how you envision your days after you stop working.

Have you considered how your spending can increase? If you already have a plan for the distribution phase, do you think it can handle your idea of how you want to spend your free time? Or would it cover unexpected medical expenses?

In the next chapter, we'll explore solid, actionable strategies to maintain and boost your retirement income. This chapter will cover the ins and outs of making your retirement savings stretch further, adapting to retirement life's financial fluctuations. Let's move on and get one step closer to turning your retirement goals into reality.

Chapter Three

Bridging the Gap Part 2: Strategies to Maintain and Increase Retirement Income

Not everyone enjoys the volatility like Alex from our last story. As the golden years approach, the appeal of risk-taking starts to diminish for many. It's something I've seen time and again in my career. The thought of retirement should bring a sense of calm, but for many people, it's the opposite. They find themselves experiencing stress thanks to the unpredictable nature of the stock market. Frequently, many retirees worry about the anxiety from the market's constant swings. This ongoing concern affects their quality of life, leaving them to wonder if there's more to retirement than just watching numbers fluctuate. The stock market still has a place in one's retirement planning.

However, we must find a balance and blend it with other strategies to generate more income during retirement.

Exploring Additional Income Sources

Discussing additional income sources beyond investing when preparing for retirement may seem unappealing. You might be saying, "Dan, I've spent decades working hard. Retirement is about relaxing, not working." While you're right, you need to make sure your Saturdays are as fulfilling as possible to keep you both happy and active. Finding joy and fulfillment in retirement can also be an opportunity to pursue passions and even generate income alongside it. You can adjust your daily routine in ways that bring purpose and even add a little extra income.

A relevant example is from a client, a former office worker who always dreamed of the day he could leave desk life. He reached retirement at 62 with a substantial pension and social security to support him. He had a love for plants, so he started working at a local nursery a few days a week. It was simple at first, but he became passionate about it, developing expertise in the local plants. People appreciated his advice. His part-time job quickly turned into something special, showing us all that finding a bit of work you love doing can enhance retirement.

The beauty of this stage in life is that you have the freedom to choose. No more boss, no more deadlines for tasks you're not passionate about, just opportunities that bring satisfaction and fit into your ideal retirement lifestyle. Imagine leveraging those years of hard-earned experience without the demands of a 9-to-5. Think of retired nurses sharing their wisdom as consultants or CPAs offering their financial expertise flexibly. These aren't just jobs; they're extensions of your passions, providing purpose and, yes, a welcome income stream without tying you down.

In order to consider an agenda like this for your retirement, there are a few questions you need to ask yourself: What skills or hobbies have you always wished you could explore further? Could your years of experience in a particular field open doors to consulting, mentoring, or even a part-time position that doesn't feel like work? How does the idea of blending a bit of work with plenty of leisure sound to you?

Retirement is the perfect time to blend passion with profit, turning what you love into a source of income. Whether it's teaching, crafting, consulting, or even turning a hobby into a small business, the possibilities are as diverse as your interests.

However, not everyone's interested in the idea of working through what's supposed to be their hard-earned leisure years, even if it's pursuing a passion. And that's perfectly okay. There's another route to financial peace without working, and it's something I've seen work wonders for many folks I've had the pleasure of guiding into retirement: annuities.

Reliable Retirement Income Security

Annuities are like a dependable source of income. This is your guaranteed income stream to cover all your needs. Imagine this: every first of the month, consistently, a payment lands in your account. This is your guarantee to cover housing, insurance, groceries, the occasional night out and just about everything that makes up the fabric of your daily life, which is, believe it or not, guaranteed for life. This kind of security brings more than just financial comfort; it brings peace of mind.

However, as we all know, living costs have a tendency to increase over time, thanks to the reality of inflation. Being prepared for this means adding a bit of strategic planning.

Think of it as having a backup annuity, a safety net you can activate whenever you need that extra boost to keep up with the rising cost of expenses. It's like having a financial safeguard, ensuring that your purchasing power stays strong, year after year. However, finding the right annuities isn't always straightforward. Some of them come with hidden fees and terms that aren't exactly in your favor. So, you've got to be vigilant for those and make sure you're picking the ones that truly work for you without any surprises hidden in the details.

Over the years of working with clients, I have come to understand that not all life insurance and annuity companies are managed the same way or with the same focus on "Transparency, Surplus & Riskier Assets (TSR)." Here is where I add more value to my clients, as I only use insurance and annuity companies with an excellent TSR rating.

I use the TSR rating because private equity firms buy insurance companies and convert them into stock companies. This means they are motivated to generate higher returns for their shareholders rather than prioritizing policyholders as mutual insurance companies do. To satisfy stockholders and drive up stock prices, these companies often invest in high-yield, high-risk assets like heavily leveraged real estate deals. TSR uses each company's own annual sworn statement to identify issues with troubled reinsurance and excessive risk relative to their stated surplus. I rely on the TSR rating for peace of mind and review these ratings annually for my clients.

Now, I'm not saying annuities are the complete solution. They're part of a broader strategy that might include long-term care, permanent life insurance and even the stock market to generate income and protect the retirement vision you've worked so hard to achieve. It's about creating a balance, a safety net that allows you to live your retirement on your terms without the worry of financial instability.

Balancing Growth and Security In Retirement

For seniors who are no longer living on employment income and rely on their savings and investments for retirement income, Smart Stocks can be a suitable option. These stocks allow you to invest in a mix of stable, income-generating assets such as 3-month T-Bills, government bonds and reliable dividend-paying stocks. This approach helps mitigate the risks often associated with the stock market's volatility.

I understand that the thought of investing in the stock market might make you cautious, especially when you're relying on your investments for retirement income. However, I recommend a balanced approach. Consider allocating a portion of your retirement investment portfolio, say 10-25%, to these stable and consistent income-generating stock positions. The key is to let experienced professionals handle it for you. That's where we come in. We're here to guide you toward reputable wealth management firms that know you by name and understand your retirement goals and aspirations.

Our investment philosophy is more focused on achieving steady, reliable returns over the long term rather than pursuing unsustainable, high-risk, high-reward opportunities. We navigate the market's fluctuations with the aim of securing a comfortable 7% return instead of chasing unrealistic 18% expectations.

It's important to note: the average person often sees a meager 4% return, falling into the pattern of buying high and selling low. That's reactionary investing, not the retirement strategy you want to be following. Also, sometimes, big investment houses are more like large ships than nimble boats—turning them around quickly isn't exactly their forte, which can leave you, the smaller investor, in a difficult position. Make sure you review all aspects of this and follow your instincts alongside your advisors.

With stockbrokers at large stock market companies who may be pressured to hit their monthly numbers, sometimes they make their investment choices based on today's bonus incentives or financial products pushed onto them by upper management. This all happens at the expense of what's generally best for you. That's why it pays to choose someone who has your back and puts your financial well-being ahead of their next commission check.

So, what's the key takeaway? It's about finding that balance between the potential of growth and the comfort of security. Blending those guaranteed income sources like annuities that are carefully chosen and organized for a senior client can ensure that even if the market decides to experience volatility, your retirement income plans remain unshaken. This allows you to enjoy your golden years with the peace and prosperity you've earned.

A relevant example: In many states with high levels of seniors, general care doctors pass their senior clients onto senior care specialists. These general care doctors understand that seniors need specialized care. Unfortunately, this doesn't happen naturally with the transition from an accumulation of retirement assets to the distribution phase of retirement assets.

Crafting a Life of Choice

So, whether you're eager to dive deep into a passion, turning that into a bit of extra cash, exploring the market's ups and downs for a slice of the investment pie, or leaning on the solid ground of annuities for peace of mind, there's a whole world of possibilities out there, ready to bridge that income gap and keep your retirement secure through the golden years of your life. With the right professional, you're all set to navigate retirement, doing everything you've ever wanted with peace of mind and contentment.

"The only way to enjoy anything in this life is to earn it first."

Ginger Rogers

Chapter Four

Smart Planning for a Prosperous Retirement

Through all the stories in this book, we've seen how much of a difference the right plan can make as you go through retirement. Speaking of the years after work, the author Tom Hegna has an interesting way of breaking down retirement into three phases: the Go-Go Years, the Slow-Go Years, and the No-Go Years, each bringing its own financial needs and opportunities. This view helps us see retirement in a clearer and more organized way, with different stages.

In the Go-Go Years, you're all set to hit the road, travel, and do everything you've dreamed of. As we said in our previous chapter, these are the years full of Saturdays. This is when spending can spike because you're making the most of your freedom.

Then come the Slow-Go Years, when health might start to slow you down a bit. This is when your spending might shift more towards healthcare and you might need to adjust your lifestyle a bit. And the No-Go Years, they can be tricky. This is when healthcare costs can go up and it's important to have a plan so these costs don't waste your savings. Understanding these stages comes in handy to plan and control your spending. Knowing what's coming can help you prepare better, ensuring your retirement is as enjoyable as possible.

I could spend another two or three pages diving into financial jargon and walking you through ideas to raise your awareness of how much the unpredictability of life can strike your plans. But as you have already noticed, I like telling the stories of people around me in my career whom I have been able to help. With that said, I want to share the example of a third couple I was fortunate to work with and help them turn a complicated situation into a simplified solution.

Turning Tides: Linda and Joseph's Retirement Reboot

I first met Joseph and Linda during one of my IRMAA seminars at Daytona Beach. They are both 55 years old and just a few years shy of paying off their home. They were unprepared for a complicated family crisis, using part of their retirement savings for their nephew's college tuition. These two spent decades saving a significant portion of their earnings because they had always wanted to use their retirement years to make some wishes and dreams come true, like international trips and a vacation home. They were both healthy and happy in their careers. They were not afraid of challenging themselves and were eager to extend their working years if it meant securing their plans.

After they reached out to me, we thoroughly examined their finances together. I laid out a plan that showed them how, by increasing their savings now, they could make up for lost time and keep enjoying life without missing a beat. We talked about prudent investments and the necessity of an emergency fund. We ran a comprehensive review of their financial landscape, laying everything on the table. This wasn't about short-term solutions. Instead, we focused on building a robust foundation for the long haul.

First, we addressed their approach to saving. I showed them how, by setting aside a more significant portion of their income now, they could accelerate their savings without sacrificing the quality of their current lifestyle. They were initially concerned about changing some comfortable habits, like dining out often or canceling a trip to see some of their family members on the East Coast that year. However, they were committed and had their eyes on their goal.

Another step we took was to explore the world of investments with a cautious eye, aiming to address their financial requirements after the crisis and prepare for future ones. We explored conservative investment strategies that promised stability and growth, albeit at a steadier pace. This decision addressed their desire to make up for lost time without taking excessive risk.

Given their past experience, emergency funds were another cornerstone of our plan. We talked about the importance of having a safety net, a reserve they could turn to without derailing their retirement savings. This wasn't just about covering unexpected expenses; it was about peace of mind.

Flexibility and long-term security were the guiding principles of our roadmap. By introducing Linda and Joseph to a variety of tax-efficient saving options, we ensured their hard-earned money worked as efficiently as possible. This wasn't about avoiding taxes at all costs, but smart planning to minimize their impact legally and effectively.

Fast forward to today, they are 69, and their situation has significantly improved. They've built a solid nest egg that got them to retirement on their terms, full of confidence. They continued their efforts; they thought about the future, about leaving something behind for their kids.

I like telling their story because it is a good example of focus and dedication. Have you ever imagined that family disagreements and problems could affect you financially? Understandably, many people can't see themselves saying no to a family member in need, especially with a nephew going into his college years. In their case, they recovered with their perseverance and openness to change with expert advice and a written plan. How would you act in their situation?

Inflation Kicker Accounts

Now, let's talk about one of the effective strategies for Linda and Joseph's retirement: Inflation Kicker Accounts. These aren't your ordinary savings accounts. They're specialized accounts that grow over time, specifically designed to keep up with the rising cost of living. Here's how these accounts helped Linda and Joseph stay ahead:

Choosing the Right Inflation Kicker Account

To begin, we looked for wise places to invest their money to grow enough to outpace inflation. We leaned towards 3-4 tax-advantaged fixed indexed annuities that grow with the market and can be turned on when inflation has negatively affected your guaranteed monthly income's ability to meet your monthly living expenses. We plan to turn on these accounts at 5-year intervals when you need more income to cover your monthly living expenses. Over time, inflation will eat away at your monthly cost-of-living expenses, so we plan for this and let these accounts grow over time until you need to turn them on and increase your monthly retirement income.

You will hear me say, "Plan Like You'll Live to 100" frequently as most people retire at age 65 and need to plan for a 35-year retirement.

1. **Timing Is Everything:** The key with these Inflation Kicker Accounts isn't to use them right when you retire but to let them grow both before and sometimes even during retirement. Due to possible tax issues, you wait until you need to tap into them, especially when the cost of living starts climbing. This way, Linda and Joseph could withdraw just the right amount to keep their comfortable lifestyle continuing without dipping too much into their main savings.

2. **Smart Withdrawals:** We carefully planned how to withdraw money from these accounts over time while letting them increase replacement funds if applicable. The idea was to use it as a top-up to their regular income whenever prices started to jump. This way, they could keep up with inflation without quickly depleting their retirement fund.

3. **Staying Flexible:** The advantageous thing about this plan was its flexibility. As life and the economy

change, so do their investments. This adaptability meant Linda and Joseph could stay comfortable, knowing they were ready for whatever the economy threw at them.

Incorporating Inflation Kicker Accounts into your retirement planning can be the turning point to ensure you've got a solid foundation for the future. Here's what makes them so valuable:

1. **Staying Ahead of the Cost of Living:** These accounts ensure you can still afford the lifestyle you love, no matter how prices rise over the years. By aligning your savings with investments that grow with or outpace inflation, you're essentially safeguarding your ability to buy what you need and enjoy what you love.

2. **Minimizing Risks:** Diversifying with assets that historically beat inflation means you're not just sitting on a pile of cash losing value each year. It's about strategically placing your investments in areas that offer both growth and a buffer against economic shifts, helping to ensure that you won't run short down the line.

3. **Feeling Secure:** Knowing you have a plan that actively combats inflation can provide peace of mind. It's one thing to save for retirement, but it's another to plan for those savings to work effectively throughout your entire retirement. This approach lets you relax and enjoy your golden years, confident that you're prepared for what the economy throws your way.

What I like about Inflation Kicker Accounts is that they're proactive. Not only can they stash your money away, but they can also make it work smarter for you. They ensure that it grows at a pace that keeps you ahead of inflation. This is a lifesaver for someone looking for a way to protect their savings from market volatility.

The Importance of Trust: How the Non-Financials Affect the Financials

Speaking of proactiveness, we must have a conversation about health, retirement and growing older. Managing finances, healthcare and making decisions gets more complicated as we age. This is a time when bringing a trusted family member into the fold of our retirement planning becomes necessary. This move ensures that the decisions affecting our health and well-being reflect what we truly want.

Starting this conversation involves picking someone—be it a family member or an advisor—who's trustworthy and understands the full picture of what you hope to achieve with your finances and health care. This person acts on your behalf when you might not be in a position to do so yourself. They make sure your voice is heard loud and clear. This is why it's essential for someone who knows you well to be involved. The sooner this trusted individual is included, the better. This allows them to fully understand your financial strategy and personal wishes, ensuring they align with your values and vision for the future.

Also, legal documents, like powers of attorney for finances and health care, establish this arrangement. They might seem like a mere formality at first glance, but they are essential tools that ensure your chosen advocate can make decisions recognized by banks, hospitals, and other institutions. As life evolves, so should these plans and documents, ensuring they always reflect your current wishes and circumstances.

And then, there's something called "Living Benefits Riders"—a safety net within your insurance policies. These living benefit riders can be a lifeline, allowing you to access up to 90% of the death benefit if you face a terminal illness. With chronic illnesses or a critical illness or critical injury, you can get accelerated benefits. These living benefits help create a hedge of protection and control over your life. It's a way to achieve some financial support when it's most needed, easing the burden of medical expenses or living costs during tough times.

A Future Well Planned

Getting to the end of another chapter, I hope you don't feel this has to be a heavy burden. From the cautionary tale of Linda and Joseph to this conversation about planning for a world where you might be unable to make your own decisions, it can be a bit tough, and I completely understand. But here's the thing: planning for your future is just another way to show you care for yourself and your loved ones. The silver lining in all of this is that you don't need to be an expert in every retirement strategy we've talked about, from Inflation Kicker Accounts to Living Benefits Riders. I am prepared to work with you. I will listen to your needs for your retirement vision and help make it a reality. To work with you, understand what you're looking for in your retirement, and help make it happen.

"Retirement is a blank sheet of paper. It is a chance to redesign your life into something new and different."

Patrick Foley

Chapter Five

Protecting Retirement Income from Taxes

Having talked about the importance of a well-thought-out retirement income plan, let's shift our focus to a subject that might not seem appealing but is essential for retirement planning.

Let's look at it in a new light: Instead of seeing it as a significant obstacle, think of it as an opportunity to protect your finances now and in the future. The methods we're about to explore come from working closely with tax-reducing advisors, CPAs and experts nationwide. Their combined expertise guides us towards a retirement that is compliant with the law and effectively manages taxes for better efficiency.

The Art of Transforming Tax-Deferred into Tax-Advantaged

One of the strategies we use regarding taxes is to move your money from accounts like 401(k)s and IRAs, where it's taxed later, into places where it can grow tax-free. The idea is to use a system where you get a tax credit for every dollar you move. This credit covers the taxes you would have paid, so you're not losing out. By the time you're ready to use your retirement funds, you've set them up to grow without being diminished by taxes.

Let's take a closer look at a strategic move you can make with your retirement savings: If you use some of your retirement money that hasn't been taxed yet to buy insurance that covers long-term care, you won't pay taxes on that money at all. Why is this beneficial? It's a way of ensuring that the money you're saving now is worth more in the future because you're not handing over a portion in taxes. This strategy makes every dollar work harder for you and ensures that when you need to rely on your savings, they're as robust as they can be.

Simplifying Complexity: Making Tax Planning Understandable

In the first pages of this book, I promised to provide simple explanations and guides. So, keeping that in mind, my approach to clarifying complex tax concepts for my clients is straightforward: show, don't just tell. Through real-world examples and having content experts on call, I ensure my clients grasp the strategies we discuss and see their potential impact. Whether explaining the nuances of a 401(h) retirement healthcare plan or the benefits of an 831(b) plan for managing taxable income, the objective is always clarity and empowerment.

As I have mentioned before, I prefer to use stories to illustrate my points instead of delving into detailed explanations. This time, instead of a couple, our main character is Alex. He became my client years ago, and his story serves as an instructive example of the effectiveness of strategic planning and the importance of making informed decisions.

A Group Effort Against Taxes

From what I know, Alex has always been a hardworking individual with a knack for entrepreneurship. He had built a successful business empire before he was 50 and managed to live the comfortable life that many desired. However, his good business decisions and strategies were not enough to keep him from being hit by a hefty tax bill. One day, he faced a taxable income of four million dollars. He was already using standard tax-minimization strategies but decided it was time to look for experts to minimize that bill. That's when we met.

Three days after our first online interaction, we had a virtual meeting. We discussed his financial situation and I introduced him to the 401(h) plan—a plan similar to the 401(k) but for healthcare costs in retirement. Alex was interested and surprised no one had told him about it before. To expand our knowledge and help him, I contacted John, an expert in retirement healthcare planning, who joined us through a video call. With his years of experience, John explained the 401(h) plan in simple terms, showing how it could help Alex save on taxes by setting aside money for future healthcare expenses. This could reduce his taxable income significantly, which caught Alex's attention.

Encouraged by this, we then looked at the 831(b) plan, another less common strategy for managing taxable income. I brought in Roger, known for his expertise in tax strategies, to explain the benefits. Roger's explanation showed how the 831(b) plan could improve Alex's tax situation and give him more control over his finances. In one of our many phone calls after we met for the first time, Alex mentioned that deciding to embrace the strategies when he reached out for help was a turning point in his life. This type of feedback fills me with satisfaction and a sense of accomplishment. It makes me remember my father and my purpose in helping people throughout the country (RIP Russell Morris).

But, aside from personal fulfillment and helping one more client protect his hard-earned money from taxes, I want to point out the importance of a team effort in a complex task such as this scenario. Whenever I faced a question that stretched beyond my expertise, I knew exactly who to turn to on my team. This network of seasoned professionals—each an expert in their own right—ensures that my clients, like Alex, are never left without answers or innovative solutions. This philosophy of collaboration and access to a broad spectrum of knowledge truly transforms how my clients view and plan for their retirement.

Common Pitfalls in Retirement Tax Planning

Stories like this make it more evident that tax strategies aren't exactly the easiest part of planning. Despite the best intentions, some retirees encounter common traps that can derail their goals. Here's a look at these pitfalls and how to avoid them, drawing insights from Alex's path.

First, not having a concrete retirement income plan is a surprisingly common oversight. Without it, many retirees find themselves uncertain, unsure how to manage their savings effectively, potentially leaving their financial security to chance. Another misstep involves over-relying on tax-deferred accounts like 401(k)s and IRAs without a plan for tax-efficient withdrawals. Initially, Alex faced this very scenario. However, diversifying his savings into tax-free avenues significantly improved his financial outlook. This approach is the best fit for anyone looking to safeguard their savings and maintain a consistent income in retirement.

Lastly, overlooking the role of insurance in retirement planning can be a critical oversight. Whether for long-term care or life coverage, insurance acts as a safety net, protecting against unforeseen expenses that could otherwise deplete one's retirement funds. Alex's proactive decision to secure long-term care insurance with tax-deferred money exemplifies the strategic use of resources to fortify one's financial future. Recognizing the importance of insurance is essential for preserving your hard-earned savings and ensuring your peace of mind throughout retirement. Retirees can take proactive steps to ensure their financial stability by understanding and avoiding these pitfalls, much like Alex did.

Staying Ahead: Continuous Learning and Expert Collaboration

All of my passion, expertise and hard work with retirement planning come down to one powerful idea: keep learning and team up with the best in the business. This combination of staying current on the latest in taxes and financial planning, plus working with top experts, isn't just something I do—it's what makes all the difference. I'm fully committed when it comes to keeping up with tax changes and new strategies in the financial world. Having a network of trusted pros, like those who helped Alex sort out his finances, means I've always got the best advice at my fingertips. This approach ensures that advice comes from a place of deep understanding and real-world expertise.

I imagine that by now, you have a clearer understanding of the critical role tax planning plays in securing a financially stable retirement. My goal was to spark your interest in seeking the right guidance to navigate these waters. Looking ahead, we'll explore another vital aspect of retirement planning. In our next chapter, we'll break down the basics of Medicare and how IRMAA impacts your healthcare expenses. Understanding these elements is key to effectively managing your healthcare costs and avoiding common pitfalls that can affect your retirement savings.

Chapter Six

Medicare and IRMAA: Navigating Healthcare Traps in Retirement

Throughout my career, I've had the chance to assist people all over the United States. Not too long ago, I found myself helping Martha, who lived in Sarasota, Florida. Martha was enjoying the calm of her retirement mornings, something she'd worked hard for her entire life. Her cozy three-bedroom home was her retirement haven. But then, one November day, as she was going through her mail with her morning coffee, she encountered an issue.

The letter from the Social Security Administration surprised her. It said she owed $1,353 in Medicare premiums and her usual $527 in Social Security benefits would stop in December to cover what she owed over her financial and tax return details. Martha was shocked. She thought she had everything organized to avoid surprises like this.

As she started looking for help, she eventually called me after a mutual acquaintance referred her to me. Feeling stressed, she gave me a call. Her voice was filled with worry as she filled me in. Immediately, it became clear that, just like in James and Clara's story, Martha had just moved over into a higher IRMAA bracket by a mere $701 last year, a small oversight from her CPA that caused a big impact.

I suggested we involve her CPA and thoroughly examine her financial details. The plan was to carefully review her financial situation and identify any overlooked tax deductions that could adjust her income by $702 and amend her tax return. It wouldn't be easy, but after collaborating for a few months, we managed to resolve the issue. Martha's story is like James and Clara's and many others throughout our country. The frequency with which people encounter this situation makes it more necessary to keep a close eye on the details in retirement planning, especially with Medicare and IRMAA surcharges and Social Security income on the line.

Sharing her experience is important to me because it really shows the kind of unexpected challenges healthcare can throw at you. With that said, let's explore avoiding these healthcare obstacles and ensure your retirement savings aren't negatively impacted by surprises.

Beyond Premiums: The IRMAA Effect on Retirement Income

Now it's finally time to explore the concept of IRMAA, which I have been talking about many times in this book. As you probably know by now, IRMAA stands for Income-Related Monthly Adjustment Amount. It is a critical yet often overlooked aspect of retirement planning that, at its core, is an additional fee you pay on top of your Medicare Part B (Medical) and Part D (prescription drugs) premiums. Medigap policies help pay some of the health care costs that the Original Medicare Plan doesn't cover. Many of my clients, much like Martha, James, Clara and others, were initially unaware of these thresholds, let alone the fact that the President of the United States has the power to adjust these levels, potentially affecting their retirement funds significantly. It's important to note that the money collected from IRMAA surcharges doesn't directly support Medicare but goes into the broader government funds.

To put this into perspective, imagine you're planning a road trip with a budget for fuel. Now, imagine the government can suddenly increase fuel taxes based on how far you're driving. If you're unaware of these potential increases, you could run out of funds sooner than expected. This is similar to what can happen with IRMAA – it's an additional expense that can surprise you if you're not prepared.

In Martha's case, just a small miscalculation in her income and a CPA who wasn't considering the ramifications put her over the threshold, leading to an unexpected IRMAA surcharge. This highlights the importance of precise income planning in retirement. Utilizing specialized software, I work with clients to protect their retirement income and assess potential IRMAA charges, forming strategies to mitigate these costs wherever possible.

Surprisingly, many financial advisors and CPAs lack a deep understanding of IRMAA despite its introduction in 2003. Many assume the income brackets are too high to affect most of their clients, a misconception that could lead clients to costly errors like we've seen with the stories I told. As the government seeks ways to address its continuing deficits, changes to these income brackets could become a reality, impacting even those who believed they were safely below the threshold.

Also, the disparity between the cost-of-living adjustments, which average around 3.2% and the annual 7% increase in Medicare costs poses a substantial risk to retirees' financial health.

To illustrate, let's revisit Martha's scenario: if her Social Security benefits are her primary source of income, the rising Medicare costs could eventually consume her entire Social Security payment. This alarming possibility underscores the importance of being proactive and well-informed about these potential charges.

In other words, the ever-changing landscape of retirement planning means that one may pay into Social Security in one's later years instead of receiving it.

This scenario, which remains unknown for most, emphasizes the need for a strategic approach to retirement income. By understanding and planning for IRMAA and the potential for rising healthcare costs, we can better protect our financial future and ensure that our retirement years are as secure and enjoyable as we've envisioned.

Smart Solutions for Healthcare Costs

Here's how we can address rising healthcare costs effectively, ensuring your retirement savings are well-protected:

1. **Embrace a Healthy Lifestyle:** "Health is wealth" is more than just a saying; it's a practical strategy for reducing future Medicare costs. Leading a healthy lifestyle, ideally with the guidance of a nutritionist or a health professional, can decrease the likelihood of medical issues that lead to high Medicare expenses. Simple changes in diet, regular exercise and preventive healthcare can go a long way to maintaining your well-being and, consequently, keeping your healthcare costs in check.

2. **Opt for Comprehensive Medicare Coverage:** With Medicare costs expected to climb by 7% annually, outstripping the Social Security [1] COLA increases, thorough coverage is essential. Ensuring you have Part B, D and especially Medicare Gap

---

1. Cost-Of-Living Adjustments - Since 1975, Social Security's general benefit increases have been based on increases in the cost of living, as measured by the Consumer Price Index.

insurance can provide you with peace of mind. Medicare Gap insurance, such as Plan G, Plan N and High Deductible Plan G, acts as a financial safeguard against the potentially significant costs of an unexpected hospital stay, covering expenses that regular Medicare does not. These plans offer various levels of coverage and can be a cost-effective solution to meet your healthcare needs.

3. **Plan for Long-Term Care Needs:** The chance you'll need long-term care isn't something to ignore. And let me tell you, the price tag attached to it can really impact your finances. Unfortunately, many people who find themselves needing long-term care won't have too many years ahead of them. That's why having a strategy is non-negotiable. It is necessary to make an educated estimate on what you might need down the line and include the coverage costs in your plan. That will keep your finances protected from the substantial care costs, whether in a high-end facility or the comfort of your home.

4. **Explore Medicare with Guidance:** The Medicare insurance landscape is diverse, with poli-

cies varying widely by county. This complexity makes finding the right coverage for your needs challenging. However, as you already know, you don't have to do this alone. Consider partnering with someone who has a deep understanding of the market. As someone deeply immersed in these matters, I offer my expertise to guide you through the Medicare options, ensuring you secure the most beneficial and cost-effective coverage.

Now, if you read stories I told here, like Martha's, and are afraid you might be unprepared soon, we can have a no-fee exploratory call via Zoom. During this session, we will discuss your specific needs and concerns. I can also provide you with specific information on how to acquire your IRMAA report. Schedule your call at 386-675-0001

Now that you are among the few Americans who are aware of IRMAA's surcharges and other possible pitfalls from the healthcare industry, I want to take you to the next and final chapter in our learning process. In the next pages, I will explore more about other aspects of healthcare and how to make the most of your Social Security benefits. We'll examine strategies to boost your retirement income, building on the secure foundation we've discussed here.

Chapter Seven

Supercharging Income: Maximizing Social Security Benefits

Even though we are approaching the end of this book, I want to make sure my promise of keeping complicated ideas simple stands strong. As we explore more specific ideas and strategies, I will explain the importance and workings of maximizing your Social Security benefits. Firstly, it's essential to understand that while Medicare provides valuable health coverage for retirees, it's not entirely free. Medicare Part A covers hospital stays and is typically premium-free for those who have paid Medicare taxes while working. However, Medicare Part B (outpatient services) and Part D (prescription drugs) do come with monthly premiums that vary based on your income.

Using Tech to Avoid "Reduced Income" Surprises

As we covered in previous chapters, IRMAA can surprise you when you least expect it if you aren't well-prepared. We minimize this probability by using specialized software to run IRMAA calculations. We can assess how your retirement assets and projected income might place you within the IRMAA brackets. This initial analysis prevents our clients from getting that undesired letter informing them of a bracket change, like what happened with Martha. The software can also be useful when diversifying your income sources during your retirement years. Certain income sources, such as withdrawals from tax-deferred accounts, can increase your taxable income, potentially pushing you into a higher IRMAA bracket, and that result can be predicted and prevented.

Practical Steps and Considerations

1. Review and Plan Income Sources: Look at your retirement income sources and understand how they might affect your IRMAA bracket placement. This includes everything from IRA withdrawals to part-time work.

2. Consider Timing of Withdrawals: Timing can be crucial. For example, large withdrawals over multiple years or considering Roth IRA conversions can help manage your taxable income.

3. Stay Informed on Bracket Changes: Since the IRMAA brackets can change, staying informed about these changes is important. Adjustments to the brackets can affect your planning and strategies for minimizing IRMAA charges.

To incorporate IRMAA into your Medicare cost planning, you're taking a comprehensive approach to managing healthcare expenses in retirement. The key is understanding how your income impacts those costs and how you can mitigate them.

Morning Run: A Twist of Fate

For the last story of this book, I want to share a client's story that can serve as a cautionary tale of how life can change suddenly for us and how much better things could be if we prepared for it. This client is John, a 69-year-old who used to pride himself on his good health and active lifestyle.

He was well-known in his neighborhood for his daily runs and community involvement. Every day, like clockwork, he would get up early in the morning and jog around the neighborhood. One of these mornings started with the last drops of persistent rain that lasted the entire night. As usual for that time of the year, he checked if the rain had stopped, got his gear, and went for one more jog. However, that day, when he was just a couple of hundred yards from home, he misstepped on the curb and fell down. That wasn't the first time it happened; for him, it certainly wouldn't be the last. So, he picked up his phone from the grass, cleaned up the wet dirt from his jacket and continued his way home, not thinking much of the incident at the time.

Shortly after, John noticed troubling changes. His usually sharp memory started failing him over trivial things, leading him to seek medical advice. An MRI revealed a major concussion from his fall, explaining the sudden change in his memory.

As his condition worsened, he had to stop his jogging sessions as walking became a struggle and his independence was at stake. Eventually, John was hospitalized for his safety, marking the beginning of a challenging recovery period. John started recovering after being hospitalized for 90 days.

His motor skills slowly started to return. With the help of specialized professionals, he recovered his ability to walk in a few months. And now, he is on his way to restarting his old habit of jogging through the streets.

The ending of John's story might have filled you with relief. And yes, he is fully recovered and do you know why? John had the foresight to secure Medigap insurance. That one decision to purchase Medigap saved him from having to deal with a bill of $787,000. Thanks to his proactiveness, all he had to pay was $2,780; everything else was covered.

Now, considering your current plan regarding medical expenses during retirement, how much would you have to pay if something like this happened tomorrow?

My intention in sharing this story is not to cause concern, I just want to emphasize the importance of planning for medical expenses during your retirement years. I want you to know that having this peace of mind is within your reach. With the right preparation, we can face unpredictable health issues without compromising our financial security.

Simplifying Social Security Benefits

Now that I have made a compelling point about the importance of planning for medical expenses, I want to focus on Social Security benefits. This is a significant piece of the retirement income puzzle, and when you get a good understanding, it can really boost your financial security as you retire. Understanding Social Security's ins and outs and using effective strategies can make a big difference in your benefits.

It's a common misunderstanding that Social Security benefits are the same for everyone. Not true. What you end up with depends on how long you've worked, when you decide to start taking benefits and how you deal with IRMAA surcharges. Yes, those IRMAA fees linked to your income can affect your Medicare Part B and Part D premium costs significantly.

Managing IRMAA surcharges means getting strategic with your retirement income. It's about analyzing your income sources and making informed decisions on withdrawals to keep you in the more favorable IRMAA brackets. This strategy can help manage the costs associated with various Medicare Gap plans, such as Plan G, Plan N and

High Deductible Plan G, ensuring that you maintain comprehensive and cost-effective coverage.

Customizing your retirement strategy is key because everyone's situation is unique. Starting with an in-depth look through IRMAA impact reports helps us spot the best opportunities to adjust your retirement income, aiming to reduce IRMAA costs. For example, deciding when to take Social Security benefits is crucial. Waiting can increase your monthly benefits and give you a better cushion against rising healthcare costs. Plus, looking into options like Roth IRA conversions might provide tax-free income later, reducing your IRMAA surcharges even further.

The value of expert advice in navigating these retirement decisions can't be overstated. For instance, bringing in a Medicare Insurance Broker ensures you get the full picture of your options, their benefits and costs. Tailored advice like this is crucial for making the best choices for your retirement goals and financial situation, paving the way for a retirement plan that's both comprehensive and informed, ready to tackle Medicare costs and IRMAA surcharges with confidence.

"The key to retirement is to find joy in the little things."

Susan Miller

Conclusion:

I truly hope you found value in reading this book as I did in writing it. Wrapping up this book is significant for me. Through the various case studies and sharing my knowledge, I aimed to fulfill the promise I set out with at the very beginning of my book.

I sincerely appreciate your commitment to reading and for spending your valuable time with this information. Each page you turned has helped me further my commitment after my Dad's passing—to guide individuals to thrive in ways I wish I could have for him.

Thank you for accompanying me on this journey and I hope to meet you soon.

Daniel Morris

"Someone's sitting in the shade today because someone planted a tree a long time ago."

Warren Buffett

Part 3
THE NEXT STEP

"The best way to pay for a lovely moment is to enjoy it."

Richard Bach

Chapter Eight

The Next Steps

I am pleased to know you are interested in ways to apply the knowledge and strategies I presented throughout the book. If you're ready to implement these concepts, I'm here to help. Comprehensive retirement planning is within your reach. You can start by connecting with me at tax-freewealth.com. Let's take this step together.

Questions? Ready to Talk?

If you have questions or are considering what to do next, that's understandable. My team and I are available to discuss your concerns with you. We're here to address any questions and explore how we can support your retirement goals. To start a conversation, simply email us at:

dan@tax-freewealth.com

Or contact us at **(386) 675-0001**. The initial phone meeting is an opportunity for us to better understand your personal income tax and IRMAA surcharge projections in retirement.

Plan for IRMAA?

As IRMAA was a big part of my book and the reason behind two of my client stories, I want to make sure your personal story won't be a cautionary tale about IRMAA surcharges in the future. For this reason, I offer my services for a personalized **IRMAA report at a discounted price of $295** when you schedule a call with me and mention my book. The IRMAA report will assist you and me, as your advisor, in better understanding your current retirement income tax projections and informing us of the future impact of Medicare premiums.

This IRMAA report will be an invaluable tool in planning to reduce unnecessary expenses that can be in the six to seven figures (that is $100k to $1m in savings over your 25–35-year retirement years).

Call me at **(386) 675-0001** or email me at **dan@tax-freewealth.com** for more information.

Partnership and Planning

What we provide is more than advice; it's an opportunity to work together based on trust and respect. Our team strives to understand your retirement goals and to align our advice with your personal objectives. If you're looking for an advisor who focuses on your needs, simplifies financial planning and supports your financial well-being, we're here for you. When you're ready to optimize your retirement planning, just let us know. We're ready to help you move towards a secure and rewarding retirement.

"The future belongs to those who believe in the beauty of their dreams."

Eleanor Roosevelt

Resources & Social Media

LinkedIn Profile

https://www.linkedin.com/in/dan-morris-/

To access my website, aim your phone camera to the QR code below and tap on the link that pops up on your screen:

Email Address

dan@tax-freewealth.com

"The best and most beautiful things in the world cannot be seen or even touched — they must be felt with the heart."

Helen Keller

About The Author

Dan Morris stands as a reference of expertise and personal dedication when it comes to retirement income planning. At 59, Dan is not just navigating the complexities of retirement planning for his clients; he's also in the prime of planning for his own future. His role as a multiple business owner and life insurance agent/broker, combined with his certification as an IRMAA Planner, uniquely positions him to author a book that delves deeply into the nuances of retirement income.

Dan's journey into retirement planning was profoundly shaped by personal experience, beginning when his father turned 61 and sought Dan's assistance. This pivotal moment sparked Dan's enduring commitment to serving seniors, a passion that has only intensified over the past 20 years. His approach is deeply personal, driven by the realization that, as he approached 50, his retirement savings were minimal due to his entrepreneurial ventures. This led to a significant shift in focus towards the distribution phase of retirement planning—a crucial yet often overlooked aspect.

A defining moment in Dan's career came while assisting his father with retirement and Medicare decisions, especially under the shadow of diabetes. This experience highlighted the critical impact of healthcare costs on retirement planning. The 2008 market crash further influenced Dan's philosophy, pivoting his strategy towards tax-free income planning for both his business and personal retirement. His discovery of the implications of IRMAA (Income-Related Monthly Adjustment Amount) on Social Security income planning in 2022 was a revelation, fundamentally integrating this insight into his practice—something that most advisors have not done.

What Dan finds most rewarding about his work in retirement planning is the deep, lasting relationships he builds with his clients, whom he considers friends. He views himself as a guardian of their retirement income plans, proactively seeking opportunities to enhance their financial well-being. This client-centric approach underscores Dan's philosophy of being an integral part of his clients' advisory teams, always staying abreast of changes that could impact their financial futures. Dan is deeply committed to his family and friends, loves restoring and repairing classic cars, is passionate about all pets and their nutrition, and, of course, retirement income planning.

I wanted to take a moment to express my heartfelt gratitude to my sweet Debbie for her invaluable assistance with my new book. Your guidance and support have truly made a significant difference in this project, and I am incredibly grateful for your love and support.

Love You!
Dan

Thanks a million for joining me on this ride and I hope to meet you soon.

Daniel Morris

Dear Reader,

Thank you for reading my book. FYI—IRMAA is part of the Social Security Administration and they contact the IRS regarding your income to determine if you are in one of the five IRMAA brackets.

The Social Security Administration (SSA) determines who pays an Income-Related Monthly Adjustment Amount (IRMAA) for Medicare Part B and Part D based on income reported on federal tax returns two years prior. The SSA uses this information to place individuals into four income brackets that determine their IRMAA. The amount of the surcharge depends on factors like income bracket and filing status.

Official IRMAA 2024 Brackets

Single	Couple MAGI	Part B	Part D
< $103,000	< $206,000	$174.70	Premium (varies)
$103,000 to $129,000	$206,000 to $258,000	$244.60	$12.90
$129,000 to $161,000	$258,000 to $322,000	$349.40	$33.30
$161,000 to $193,000	$322,000 to $386,000	$454.20	$53.80
$193,000 to $500,000	$386,000 to $750,000	$559.00	$74.20
> $500,000	> $750,000	$594.00	$81.00

The problem is that these IRMAA brackets change every year, and with the stroke of a pen, any U.S. President can change the brackets. I believe they may lower them significantly to generate more tax revenue, which means we would lose a larger part of our SS income in retirement. These IRMAA surcharges do not go into the SSA bank accounts but into the government's general accounts, which means they can use those funds for anything they wish.

Income for IRMAA

Income sources for IRMAA

Taxable Social Security benefit	Qualified Annuities
Wages	Traditional 401(k) distributions
Pension Income	Traditional IRAs distributions
Rental Income	Traditional 403(b) distributions
Capital Gains	Traditional 457 distributions
All Dividends	Traditional SEP-IRA distributions

Source: https://www.ssa.gov/OP_Home/handbook/handbook.25/handbook-2501.html

Income for IRMAA

Income that does NOT count towards IRMAA

Roth Accounts
Certain Life Insurance
Health Savings Accounts (HSA)
Specific Annuities
401(H) Plans
Home Equity

Source: https://www.ssa.gov/OP_Home/handbook/handbook.25/handbook-2501.html

I hope this helps you understand where your retirement income funds should be stored and distributed from. This is what I plan to work on with my clients. If you have any questions, please let me know.

Dear Reader,

Thank you for reading my book. FYI – Below is an example of an IRMAA report which I did as an example to show my clients. All the figures are real and the names have been changed. The IRMAA report uses the actual retirement portfolio and projects retirement income based on RMDs, income taxes, and IRMAA bracket surcharges. Most of my clients are shocked, to say the least. The #1 expense in retirement is healthcare even though we have Medicare. Contact me for more information.

Medicare IRMAA Calculator

Your projected Medicare liability: $2,483,155.49

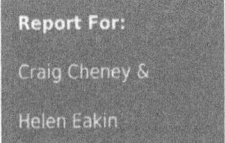

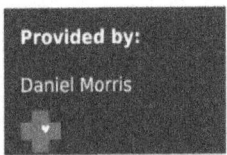

DESIGNING A TAX-SMART RETIREMENT

 Prepared for Craig Cheney & Helen Eakin

Did you know that the Rules of Retirement have changed

Through the years Congress has changed the rules of retirement in 4 distinct ways that will impact not only your financial plans, but also your health coverage and Social Security benefits.

The 4 Rules of Retirement are:

Rule 1: You have a mandatory expense in retirement

In order to receive any Social Security benefit, you must accept Medicare when eligible.

Eligibility is when you are 65-years-old or older and no longer have health coverage through an employer or spouse's employer. COBRA does NOT count.

Rule 2: Medicare is based on your income through the Income Related Monthly Adjustment Amount or IRMAA.

The more income you have, the higher your Medicare premiums.

Rule 3: Income for IRMAA is your adjusted gross income plus any tax-exempt interest you may have.

Some examples of IRMAA income: Wages, Social Security benefits, Capital Gains, Dividends and distributions from Traditional 401(k) and IRA's.

Rule 4: The bulk of your Medicare premiums and any IRMAA surcharges you have are both deducted directly from your Social Security benefit.

Did you know that Social Security's cost of living adjustment (COLA) is projected to be no greater than 2.40% from 2023 to 2030 while Medicare premiums are expected to grow by more than 6.00%?

Your Social Security benefit is not going to be what you are planning it to be

Year	Age	SSA Income	Part B	Part D	Medigap	Total Cost	Remaining SSA Income	IRMAA Bracket
2037	65	$0.00	$0.00	$0.00	$0.00	$0.00	$0.00	None
2038	66	$0.00	$0.00	$0.00	$0.00	$0.00	$0.00	None
2039	67	$42,000.00	$3,462.21	$2,746.77	$6,998.49	$6,208.98	$35,791.02	None
2040	68	$43,050.00	$3,719.45	$2,949.21	$7,578.60	$6,668.66	$36,381.34	None
2041	69	$44,126.25	$3,995.81	$3,166.57	$8,209.33	$7,162.37	$36,963.88	None
2042	70	$45,229.41	$4,292.69	$3,399.95	$8,888.21	$7,692.64	$37,536.77	None
2043	71	$46,360.14	$4,611.64	$3,650.52	$9,622.59	$8,262.16	$38,097.98	None
2044	72	$47,519.14	$4,954.29	$3,919.56	$10,414.09	$8,873.85	$38,645.29	None
2045	73	$48,707.12	$5,322.39	$4,208.44	$11,270.52	$9,530.83	$39,176.30	None
2046	74	$49,924.80	$5,717.84	$4,518.60	$12,194.39	$10,236.44	$39,688.36	None
2047	75	$51,172.92	$6,142.68	$4,851.62	$13,190.20	$10,994.30	$40,178.62	None
2048	76	$52,452.24	$6,599.08	$5,209.18	$14,265.87	$11,808.26	$40,643.98	None
2049	77	$53,763.55	$7,089.39	$5,593.10	$15,426.99	$12,682.49	$41,081.06	None
2050	78	$55,107.64	$17,420.13	$9,688.36	$16,683.20	$27,108.49	$27,999.15	1st IRMAA Bracket
2051	79	$56,485.33	$18,714.20	$10,402.39	$18,039.89	$29,116.84	$27,368.49	1st IRMAA Bracket
2052	80	$57,897.46	$20,104.93	$11,169.05	$19,506.73	$31,273.98	$26,623.48	1st IRMAA Bracket
2053	81	$59,344.90	$21,598.73	$11,992.21	$21,091.69	$33,590.94	$25,753.96	1st IRMAA Bracket
2054	82	$60,828.52	$23,203.52	$12,876.03	$22,785.84	$36,079.55	$24,748.98	1st IRMAA Bracket
2055	83	$62,349.24	$24,927.54	$13,825.00	$24,613.75	$38,752.53	$23,596.70	1st IRMAA Bracket
2056	84	$63,907.97	$26,779.65	$14,843.90	$26,589.37	$41,623.55	$22,284.42	1st IRMAA Bracket
2057	85	$65,505.67	$28,769.38	$15,937.89	$28,722.15	$44,707.27	$20,798.39	1st IRMAA Bracket
2058	86	$67,143.31	$44,165.42	$17,476.11	$31,005.21	$61,641.53	$5,501.78	2nd IRMAA Bracket
2059	87	$68,821.89	$47,446.91	$18,764.10	$33,469.68	$66,211.01	$2,610.88	2nd IRMAA Bracket
2060	88	$70,542.44	$50,972.21	$20,147.02	$36,125.17	$71,119.23	-$576.79	2nd IRMAA Bracket
2061	89	$72,306.00	$54,759.45	$21,631.85	$38,986.10	$76,391.30	-$4,085.30	2nd IRMAA

DESIGNING A TAX-SMART RETIREMENT

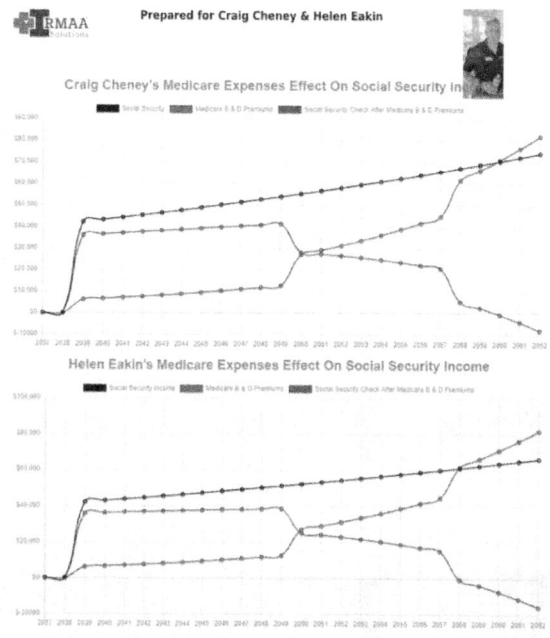

Generating the personalized IRMAA Report is just the start of my retirement income planning process. I hope this IRMAA report example motivates you to call me for your personalized IRMAA report.

If you should have any questions, please let me know.

All the best,

Dan Morris

Made in United States
Orlando, FL
02 August 2025